T0072535

THE CHILDREN OF AVALON

HOPE FOR HUMANITY

KHAMSONE LIMSAVANH

BALBOA.PRESS

A DIVISION OF HAY HOUSE

Balboa Press books may be ordered through booksellers or by contacting:

Balboa Press
A Division of Hay House
1663 Liberty Drive
Bloomington, IN 47403
www.balboapress.com
844-682-1282

Because of the dynamic nature of the Internet, any web addresses or
links contained in this book may have changed since publication and
may no longer be valid. The views expressed in this work are solely those
of the author and do not necessarily reflect the views of the publisher,
and the publisher hereby disclaims any responsibility for them.

The author of this book does not dispense medical advice or prescribe the use
of any technique as a form of treatment for physical, emotional, or medical
problems without the advice of a physician, either directly or indirectly. The
intent of the author is only to offer information of a general nature to help
you in your quest for emotional and spiritual well-being. In the event you use
any of the information in this book for yourself, which is your constitutional
right, the author and the publisher assume no responsibility for your actions.

Any people depicted in stock imagery provided by Getty Images are
models, and such images are being used for illustrative purposes only.
Certain stock imagery © Getty Images.

Print information available on the last page.

ISBN: 978-1-9822-7780-2 (sc)
ISBN: 978-1-9822-7782-6 (hc)
ISBN: 978-1-9822-7781-9 (e)

Library of Congress Control Number: 2021924457

Balboa Press rev. date: 12/08/2021

I dedicate this book to my late mother, Manivone and the children of Avalon.

Love,
Khamsone

CONTENTS

ACKNOWLEDGMENTS

My thanks go to the people who have helped me with my life, Maya and all my friends.

PROLOGUE

Her name is Melissa, and this is the story of her being reincarnated into this life as the children of Avalon. In a time when the churches crusading across the continent in search of witches, her people become their main targets and are hunted down like dogs. Finally, all the children of Avalon are caught and burnt alive.

After awakening from being human, Melissa keeps the witching part of her life hidden from the world. She possesses extraordinary gifts of power. Aa a witch, Melissa is neither good nor she is evil, but unique. She can command both of light and dark magic. However, Melissa chooses to practice only with the power of light. By divine providence, the gods are reincarnating her people back to life. This time around, the children of Avalon are the last and only hope for humanity survival. The existence of the children repels most darkness and negativity in proximities. The gods create the children and endow in them the power of angel of peace and angel of prosperity. Thus, the children are tasked with a mission to guide humanity back to the light and God. If nothing is done to change the nature of man, he will repeat his true desire and will yield to his inevitable fate of succumbing to evil. Omnes mali sunt.

CHAPTER I

---◇◈◇◈◇---

THE ARRIVAL

Around the year 2000, Melissa was born into an affluent-interracial family somewhere in North America. Having her upbringing in the way of Christian, she was happy at first. Early on, she became increasingly confused and many of her questions went unanswered. Her family were supportive and good providers, but all the while keeping their distances from her. Being the only child, Melissa was different from everyone around her. She questioned everything and everyone she came across. School was easy for Melissa, and she managed it without so much a struggle. Like everything else, popularity was not even an issue to Melissa. Everything was fine, until right after her

15th birthday. A scar magically appeared out of nowhere and embedded itself on the skin of her left shoulder. Up until then, everything of this world that she had learned and knew about was about to change in ways that it would shock her whole foundation in the coming days. Her normal life of these past 15 years was about to take a turn to a mythical proportion.

It started out as a small rash then gradually kept growing larger and larger. There was no end to it. Her mom had dermatologist checked out her shoulder and ran some tests on it. They told her the test results showed that it just a common rash and prescribed her some creams for the itching. Weeks later, the itching stopped. What remained were some dried up scabs covering part of her left shoulder area. She was spending part of the following days de-scabbing part her left shoulder one piece at a time until there was no more. When all the scabs were gone, the remained area showed reddish- brown mark embedded deep on her skin much like a birthmark. It shaped like a distorted horseshoe about three inches across. The culprit revealed itself.

As growing young teenager, Melissa had to endure and survive many teenage crises and unrelenting peer pressures. This uninvited mark on her shoulder was a problem for her and her already existing anxiety. She was suffering from a mild form of insecurity. Her family was trying hard comforting her and even going so far as claiming the mark was a new form of trend and unique. They when on assuring her that when

Melissa grew older, if necessary, she can have it removed. Like many young girls, Melissa had always look up to her mother as a great mentor, a role model, and a source of inspiration. Little that Melissa knew, this childhood predicament with the marking on her shoulder was no mere accident. In fact, it was transpired long ago before the world was at war, and before man committed atrocity against God.

The following weeks, Melissa confident level improved considerably. When she was out in publics, she sometimes flashing and wiggling her shoulder around as if daring others to notice the marking. Her mom was baffled, but at the same time amazed by Melissa carelessness. Sometimes her mother jokingly told her family about how she unknowingly created a monster out of Melissa. As the week dragged on, Melissa symptoms and fallouts with the marking were gradually subsided and eventually faded away into nothing but a distant memory. Finally, Melissa was back being herself once again, a happy growing teenage girl, so it would seem. Years later, Melissa was a senior in high school and just turning seventeen, then the cursed mark on her left shoulder returned. With it, the deep seeded burning sensation of hot boiling water being poured on the skin of her left shoulder and accompanying by vivid dreams and unrelenting nightmares. Melissa was then a beautiful young lady in her full-grown adolescent, and once again found herself back confronting her childhood nightmares that she thought were long forgotten.

AWAKENING

Her fever began to break out along with her nightmares. She started to have flashes of visions and memories of someone else that were not her own. Someone from another times and places in a distant past. Melissa could made out the clothing and styles of the individuals were from around the year 1800s and somewhere in England. As time when on, these experiences were starting to affect Melissa and altering her personality and demeanor. For the moment, Melissa sensory perceptions were also heightened, and she began to develop psychic ability and ESP. Every passing day, her extrasensory perception and empath ability grew more intensified and overwhelming her to the point that she had to avoid any contact with others including those from her own family. Melissa had to learn how to find comfort in solitude, and that she had to avoid any unnecessary contact with others. This was hard on Melissa, especially in school.

Barely made the graduation, Melissa was relieved to find herself free from being in proximity with others, and college was not even on her immediate agenda. Melissa was trying to come to term with her new understanding of herself that she was a witch or being possessed by one. Confounded by this dilemma, Melissa had to keep it a secret from everyone and her family. A somewhat strict-Christian family, they could turn extremist against her had they learn about her being a witch. Therefore, Melissa could not have any chance of them finding out. To avoid human-negative emotions, Melissa had to put her future-academic plan on hold. She had to avoid any large gathering of people such as attending church or watching games with friends. Thus, all human contacts were suspended. Melissa had to find out what was really happening with her and how to deal with the anomalies that overwhelmed her life.

Left with no alternative, Melissa took upon herself to get rid of the mark. She tried scratching on it with her fingernails until her skin tissues starting to peel off and bleeding out with blood. To avoid further self-mutilation, she made an appointment with her dermatologist the next day. She wanted nothing to do with the cursed mark any longer. That very same night, Melissa had a visitation from God in a form of an angel. While Melissa was in her deep sleep, the angel came to her dream with a vision of warning her to stop.

"Do not tamper with the Seal," the angel admonished. "In case the Seal is damaged, I will put another Seal on top of it."

Melissa turned to look at her left shoulder and saw a light glowing shaped of a circular Seal about the size of a silver-dollar coin being placed over the old Seal. Melissa recognized that the Seal had a sacred-geometric pattern with Hebrew writings on it. As she turned back to have a look at the angel, Melissa woke up.

Bewildered, astonished, and in awe were the feelings that enraptured her as she tried to touch the marking with her right hand. She wanted to touch the divine marking that placed upon her body; she wanted to touch the hands that created her; and she wanted to touch God. But for the moment, touching the marking was more than she deserved, considering her past treatments with it. She broke out in tears and crying uncontrollably from feeling quilt stricken over how she had mistreated the holy Seal that was divinely placed on her. She continued blaming herself that she was not worthy a recipient of such divine gift.

After weeks of self-loathing dramas, her self-imposed punishment finally came to an end. She came to term and acceptance of her true self that she was no ordinary human being but blessed by God chosen to fulfill an unknown destiny.

"What now?" Melissa asked herself. "Where do I begin and how?"

Realizing the enormity of the situation, she could not afford to slip up in handling this unprecedented situation. Her priority was to find out who she was, and what made her so different that a messenger of God had paid her a visit. She reminded herself to tread carefully and confined to no one until transparency of the situation evidenced itself. Melissa was learning how to do things unconventionally while leading a double life with a mission from God.

THE SEARCH

Melissa had spent the following months hitting the books and the internet searching for anything that might be relevant to her case. While not attending college, her family left her a responsibility of taking care family business which involved her to do some small risk investments. Her family owned some conglomerate shares with corporations across the country and abroad. As a training wheel for her, Melissa had to try hard and gave her all to impress them. With perseverance and many late-night researching, her hard works paid off. She made some sound investments as if she knew in advance about the future. This too was part of her latent abilities still emerging from its sleep. With any respite from her work, she was back to her hidden agenda scouring the internet and consulting with psychics of anything to do with metaphysical world.

With her participating in the family business, her family had enjoyed much needed success and growth. Melissa continued making more sound investments and earning their trust. Eventually they left her alone and easing off on meddling with her affairs. This gave her more freedom to explore the occult side of her. Thus far, she had categorized the psychics and mediums to be somewhat unreliable and even questionable source of information. However, they were entertaining and therapeutic at time not what she was searching for in her information gathering. Melissa drove on deeper into the metaphysical world, the world of the occult. She was passing beyond the point of no return and wandering off into an uncharted territory, then by chance she came across a lonely little witch named Maya. Melissa could not have believed her luck. She connected with Maya instantly as though the two were destined to meet.

Maya was a young but a talented witch. She preferred to spend part of her day sleeping. Not that she was lazy, she was just a night person. She would be up every night until dawn meditating and manifesting her works. Part native-American Indian and part Caucasian, Maya was unique even among the community of witches. When Melissa first contact with Maya in person, Maya immediately took noticed of Melissa auric-field color as an indigo blue. This sparked Maya curiosity even more. After short introduction and formality, Maya gave a specific instruction to Melissa to try meditation and relaxation. When they parted ways, Maya told Melissa to wait for her call while Maya went to work on her own meditation.

Meditation was new and even taboo to Melissa considering her Christian background. However, Melissa had already crossed that line months ago. She had pledged to herself that if knowing the truth about herself was a sin, then a sin was worth committing. Thus, onward Melissa and sinned away.

Learning about meditation was easy, but it was unbearably difficult when Melissa tried practicing it. Nevertheless, she found something like the lotus position more suitable and conducive to her equanimity. With the blessed candle lit and the smoke from burning sage permeated the air of her room, she began with a short pray to God, the angels, and her spirit guide for guidance and protection. Melissa assumed the lotus position. However, she was having difficulty maintaining the state of calmness and relaxation. This internal conflict within her dragged on for a while, then Melissa was experiencing a symptomatic-panic attack. She abruptly broke off from her meditation and ended the session early.

Melissa was perplexed and confused to have experienced firsthand account of such phenomenon that many had described in their first attempts of meditation. She had gained an understanding that this was going to be a journey filled with bumps and obstacles along the way. First, Melissa had to accept it not as failure but a significant bump in a middle of the road. The same road that took lord Buddha six-long years to complete and obtained his enlightenment. However long it took, Melissa had to endure many hardships and obstacles along the way. The old proverb ranged through her mind, "nothing ventured, nothing gained." To gain more understanding about herself and her past, she had to venture further and deeper into the unknown and risking it all. Day by day, Melissa had to reset the process over again. And much to her chagrin, the same scenario repeated itself over again. When all her attempts seemed futile, Melissa received an encouraging news of revelation from Maya. Maya called.

It had been four days since their last conversation together. This much anticipated phone called from Maya was a turning point and a game changer for the mentally distraught Melissa. The call was brief and followed by a short instruction urging

Melissa to have a meeting with her in person. For personal reason, Maya refused to divulge any finding over the phone. The overly cautious Maya was enthusiastic and could not wait to tell Melissa in person. With all hast, Melissa rushed off to their meeting with Maya.

During their meeting, Maya apologized to Melissa for withholding important information over the phone and had to be told in person. Maya continued explaining her reasoning that the phone sent out signals to space and beyond amid not knowing who or what was listening in on them. Once again Maya had to apologize to the already confused and scared Melissa. All rantings aside, Maya confined to Melissa of her findings from her meditation.

The meeting took longer than they had anticipated, but it left Melissa in shock and speechless by the sheer magnitude of its forbidden and dangerous nature of revelation. A reason enough that Maya had to take measures to maintain her secrecy, and she strongly advised Melissa to do the same. Before Melissa left for home, she gracefully thanked Maya for her hard works and her sound advice and urging her to carry on working on her case and spared no expense. As for the financial agreement, Melissa had assured Maya that she got it covered. Furthermore, she told Maya that she had more questions for her until the next time. She just wanted to go home and to allow her times taking in all this. Maya understood and encouraged Melissa to remain strong and stayed in contact.

THE ORIGIN

According to Maya, Melissa and her soul-essence origin was not from human of planet earth. In fact, she came from a distance star far away and on the other side of cosmos. Her soul group originated from a highly evolved race of beings. Spiritual by nature, her people kept evolving and subsequently many were ascended to the state of high consciousness, an ascended being. Thus, her people enjoyed peace and prosperity for thousands of years. On the request of a Supreme Being, her soul group began their crusades across the stars. They had enjoyed many successes along the way that they caught the attention of a certain Supreme Being who had specifically requested them to the planet earth. There, her first arrival was in Israel during the biblical time. Fast forward a few centuries later in late-18-century England, she was reincarnated as a young witch belonging to a secret order that lived in a mystical island called Avalon. At the age of fifteen, she was hunted down and eventually killed by the churches.

After a week of hiatus and moping around, Melissa picked herself up and carried onward with her holy mission as born-again witch. The shocking revelation revealed to her by the indiscreet Maya left her feeling ambivalent toward herself and her distance-past incarnations. Despite her Christian upbringing, Melissa gracefully embraced her newly found concept of reincarnations and the paranormal activities of the occult world. However, there remained the enigma of her being a super witch, once upon a time, had made Melissa a reluctant follower. In truth, she possessed no real power that would identify with her as a witch. Melissa had many questions for Maya, and perhaps she needed to exercise more patient and understanding by allowing times for Maya to perform her part in shedding light into her forgotten pasts. Nevertheless, Melissa had desired this was a direction that she needed to dig deeper into herself and her soul. To accomplish it, she had to resort to meditation and mastered the control of herself. Again, the all-knowing Maya came to her rescue.

Several days had passed, and another meeting with Maya was being held. During the meeting, Maya went over her findings with Melissa and provided her much needed information detailing about Melissa-past lives. Evidently, according to Maya, someone bounded Melissa's power in the recent past life and resulting in her reincarnation of being a witch without power. Prior to that life, Melissa was born into a race of ethereal being known as a guardian angel which meant all the witches in Avalon at that time were all reincarnated from angels. Maya admitted that she had done all that she could for Melissa. There were roadblocks and protocols which protected by some powerful entities that Maya had to obeyed and not trespassing any further. Any more intrusion into Melissa's past had to be done by Melissa and only her alone. For that to happen, Melissa had to learn more about meditation.

Maya immediately identified the problem with Melissa regarding her failed attempt at meditation process. She had explained to Melissa the important of the initial phase of meditation was overcoming the logical side of her. According to Maya, logic was part of the mind and existed according to the perceptions accumulated from the surrounding of oneself through the senses. Thus, the heart and the mind were two separated existences existing in oneself. Maya had emphasized that for any decision made by the mind, the heart had to agree as well. Regardless of the outcome, a decision made without the consent of the heart would invariably resulting in regret. Furthermore, Maya had expressed disappointment with the doctrine of the church's teaching that man should not be listening to his heart for it was made from dirt and clay full of impurity whereas the bible had provided the true salvation which written by man with no heart.

Contradiction aside, Maya vehemently advised Melissa the important of maintaining balance between the heart and mind. The heart had to share existence with the mind and vice versa, like yin and yang each cannot existed without the other. Melissa had to learn how to numb all her senses before taming her logic and keeping it under control. This made possible for her to maintain balance within. Ordinary, an individual had to spend years meditating and maintaining the balance between the heart and mind to achieve the activation of Kundalini awakening. Thus, being a former guardian angel helped Melissa speeding up the process.

THE JOURNEY AND TRANSFORMATION

Business as usual for Melissa when her family checked in on her and suspected nothing out of ordinary. With the impressive amount of capitals Melissa pulled in monthly, they were impressed with her and left her alone. Therefore, she was free to pursue her own agenda. In just a few months, Maya's advice for Melissa had paid off. Finally, Melissa had triumphed over the control of her mind and was able to maintain balance within her. This was the crucial phase of her long journey of self-discovery concerning her devotion to meditation. In fact, Melissa understood meditation is the key to unlock the mysteries of her forgotten past and her dormant powers hidden deep within her. The journey for Melissa had begun.

Melissa was nineteen when she started meditating. Three years later, her Kundalini energy awoken. While she was in deep meditation, a sudden electrical energy surged up through the back of her spine with tingling sensations throughout her body. Within minutes, it was gone. The effect caused Melissa to experience the unfathomable feelings of terrifying emotions blasting at her like a force of hurricane wave after wave of endless emotions. The strange energy became integrated internally inside her body and working in tandem within her cellular structures coursing through her like an energetic snake. This energy continued to stimulate her major organs and penetrating deep into her molecular structures, her DNA. As if by design, the activation of the Kundalini energy had prompted the initiation of the pre-programming coded within her DNA. It rearranged and optimized her internal structures from her pineal gland and up to her crown chakra. The snake was preparing Melissa's body for the next stage of her evolution. Melissa was evolving and changing into her true form, a witch.

Two years later, Melissa began working as Financial Consultant to a small firm that had been reeling in many deep-pocket clients over the years. She had to appreciate the modern technology which made possible for her to acquire some necessary diplomas all online and never had to set foot in a classroom. With these diplomas and her background successes had helped Melissa landed a job with this financial firm whose portfolio were mostly investments and business acquisitions. At a young age of 25 and blessed with great beauty, Melissa quickly rosed through the rank among the junior partners and was preferred by most of the clients which creating conflicts within the group. At some point, the senior partners had to intervened and set aside the differences by appointing Melissa a new title as a Special Consultant working independently outside the group. Melissa was working from home and free to engage in her work with meditation. The senior partners were unaware that Melissa was a witch. Thus, some viewed her as goose that can lay a golden egg. Others saw a beautiful-young lady full of ambitions and aspirations to succeed. Unknown to everyone, Melissa was just pretending to work hard in trying to impress the senior partners. She already knew in advance about the outcomes of the future. As part of her special power, Melissa possessed the eye that can pierce into the future.

ENTER MANIDA

A blessing and a curse, Melissa felt it the first thing when she received the gift. Knowing about the future can be a blessing if it were a favorable outcome to her, but a curse if the outcome were unavoidably bad. Nevertheless, Melissa had to be more selective and in control when applying her prescient power in channeling the future events. Melissa was adapting and learning more about her new power. This was made possible because of her hard work and perseverance of years in practicing meditation. The results were many of her hidden powers and memories started surfacing. She remembered herself being a young witch named Manida who once lived on the mystical island called Avalon. When Melissa adopted this former name in her deep meditation session, she remembered things about her past life from the island and the tragedy that caused the catalyst of the great wars between man.

THE MARKING OF A WITCH

Melissa recalled her memory of being Manida on the island. Manida was a new member to a unique family of witches living on this mysterious island called Avalon. She had been rescued from a distant land called Laos, a landlock country in the corner of Southeast Asia. Far from home but not alone, Manida and the rest of the inhabitants were mostly of non-white people living on a mysterious island in the middle of England. The only Caucasian on the island was an old lady named Evelyn. She was the mother and protector to everyone on the island. Evelyn was an old lady of great wisdom and had a special connection to all the children born with the unique birthmark. She would search the entire world for these children and recued them before the churches had their ways with them. Everyone living on the island had a unique birthmark embedded in the middle of their backs. There were about fifty people living on the island with only a few men but mostly women and kids. All were born with these birthmarks on their backs. A witch born with this birthmark had a special connection to Avalon and possessed the ability of shapeshifting and the power to command light and dark magic, the power of the Gods. Thus, prided by the churches and had a kill order to kill on site for anyone bared this marking. For centuries, the churches had dispatched their own special units all over Europe and around the world to specifically hunt down the people with this marking regardless of status, age or gender a standing kill order to kill on site. The churches knew what they were doing and were good at it. To stop the gods from having influences in the world, the churches had to eliminate all the children of the Gods.

Manida was only 15-years old when she was burnt to death as testament to the brutality of the churches. As it happened, Melissa was just turning 15 when the marking made its appearance on her left shoulder. A sign that Melissa had to carry on with her divine mission from whence Manida had met her untimely end. Although Melissa had felt reverence and great sadness when sharing memories and a soul with an innocent girl killed before her time, Melissa could never have comprehended the true depth of pain and sorrow that Manida had endured during her final moment of agonizing death. To maintain her sanity and carry on with her sacred obligation, Melissa had to exercise some semblance of objectivity when delt with the traumatic memories of her past lives. Nevertheless, she had difficulty in finding a way to forgive the church for killing her and her entire family. Melissa had to try to bury these emotions from interfering with her ongoing development perhaps engaging in romance might be a good distraction from it all.

DESTINY

The curse for knowing the future was knowing how everything ended. As for Melissa and many of her romantic episodes, all were ended before they had begun. Despite several advancements made by many men and women, Melissa had already seen through their true intentions and was able to avoid catastrophe and other emotional entanglements. When it came to love, Melissa was idealist. She was not looking for a perfect man but one that loved her for who she was and shared with her everything, good or bad. Through these developments, Melissa had regarded all men were barbaric when approaching love. They had used love as tool or weapon to ensnare the would-be-potential mates to their environment. There, the victim would reveal a vulnerability after certain time, then they revealed their true intentions by exploiting and subjecting them to their wills. Maybe it was a bad luck or a bad timing on her part. Nevertheless, this was the nature of man that Melissa had encountered. Upon her newly discovered powers and her recovered-residual memories of her past lives, Melissa true intention toward love was to find her soul companion of whom she arrived with from her original home world.

According to her original memory, Melissa and her people were warned by the Earth Guardian that planet earth and its inhabitants (man) were inherently evil. It was so evil that it had corrupted even the sons (angels) of God. The humans of planet were descendant of Adam, the first man (Adam was the first man created by God and later betrayed God by ingesting the fruit from the tree of good and evil). For this reason, the planet earth had been in quarantine since the arrival of man. Thus, to be born a human, Melissa had to be accompanied by another soul to safeguard their long journeys into a world being surrounded by humans or by evil. Melissa understood that coming to this world meant going to certain part of hell and tried to rescue some souls of whom would be damned. For this journey, many of her people would perish and herself included. Nevertheless, everyone volunteered

Melissa first arrived in Jerusalem during the biblical time accompanied by her master, her soul companion. There, she had witnessed the horrors that had transpired by man and the true battles between good and evil. Melissa was never comfortable at being human and she spent most of her journeys searching for her own kinds. Thus, she would always manage to find her way back to her soul companion, her master. Back in her own world, Melissa true form was a giant-birdlike being and the same with her master. Her main purpose on this journey was to assist her master in his last mission on earth before returning home.

DILEMMA AND THE DARK SIDE

Although much of Melissa lost memories were recovered, some memories were more vivid than others like the latest memories from the time she had spent on Avalon. The memory of her traumatic events that had transpired there took precedence over all other memories prior to Avalon. The same was also true with her power. Melissa could only recover the light side of her power but not the dark. This meant that she was incomplete as a witch. Melissa needed the dark power to defend herself and perform other forbidden magics. Without her dark power, Melissa failed to fulfill her role as a true witch of Avalon. Nevertheless, someone powerful from her past had absorbed all her dark manas. This someone was closed and dear to her, her mother.

All began and ended with Avalon, Alpha and Omega. Melissa recalled her past memory of being Manida living on Avalon. Such that, Manida was one of the special children rescued and raised by Evelyn of Avalon. Evelyn was a matriarch and a powerful witch. Those born with the special birthmarks on their backs were all belonging to Avalon. To care for all the children and its people, Avalon took on a human form known as Evelyn who would provide and protect all just like a mother would for her children. To protect her children from the unknown, Evelyn took upon herself and absorbed all the Dark Manas from all her children and her people. In the end, she paid a hefty price for cheating on the Gods. Something went horribly wrong. Despite her self-sacrifice attempts to save her beloved children and her people, she ended up hastened their dooms. All her children and her people were killed, and Avalon vanished.

Melissa hoped of return to a full witch of Avalon had been temporary derailed by the discovery of her mother, Evelyn. Her mother was a sole responsible for the disappearance of her dark mana. This implication had set in motion the state of being in a quandary for Melissa. She had to choose going forward or staying in the past. Going forward, Melissa had to accept the fact that she can use only light magic as intended by Evelyn. This way the Gods cannot exploited her or subjugated her to their whims. Thus, Melissa would be free from the Gods and free to choose her own destiny not as a witch but something new.

Melissa had chosen to be free from her past and driven forward toward a new destiny. She had done it out of love for her mother of whom had sacrificed so much for her. Melissa was eternally grateful to Evelyn and for what she had done. However, Melissa decided to help the people of this world and guided them with the help from the lost teachings of Avalon. No longer a vengeful witch and a slave to the gods, Melissa was free to live her life in accordance with the wish of her beloved mother, Evelyn. Nevertheless, she found comfort in guiding the souls of this world without the use of her dark power. All the while, she continued searching for her lost companion, her master.

CHAPTER II

———◇◇◇◇◇◇———

AVAL⊕N

I am Beginning and Ending; I am Alpha and Omega; I am Avalon.

I am everywhere and nowhere. I do not know when I am created, but I have walked the earth for as long as I can remember since the time of the great flood. Therefore, I have seen all. My responsibility is to keep the darkness and the fallen from coming up to the surface of the earth. The earth is a prison and a home for all the darkness and the undesirable in this part of the realm. I have spent many millennia watching the world, and I have witnessed countless civilizations rise and only to fall by their own makings. In time, I too will cease to be, and no one will remember me of what I have done. I am neither good nor am I evil, but sometimes I take lives to save many. I grow weary and tired of my futile labor to quell the unending darkness. Thus, I have yearning for a long and peaceful sleep. I want to die….

The gods would not let me die. They would not grant me my death, but they have freed me from my obligation for now. I am free to do anything I want and go anywhere I please. Someday, they will come looking for me and I will be ready for them. Until then, I will enjoy my well-deserved rest.

During the period of my hiatus that which span for a few centuries, I have settled down in the British Isles. The people of this land call this place England. I have finally found a place that I can call home. In preparation for my resting place, I enchant the entire surrounding forests and place my island in the middle. The lakes surrounding my island are guarded by the sisters of vampiric mermaids. The island contains some unique features of landscapes and earth mounds with turquoise-blue-water ways coursing through it. When viewing it atop from bird's eye view, the island resembles that a marking of Avalon. There, I have slumbered for many moons and many winters. Occasionally, the gods drop by for a visit and always come with bearing gifts. The first is a wounded king. They claim that he has been battling demons and lost which causes him his mortal wound. The gods call him the Pisces King. He bares the marking of Avalon on his back, and he is one of the children of Avalon. They want him to stay on Avalon and assure him that the magic here will protect and heal him in time.

PART I

KING ALPHA

Many more winters have passed since the arrival of the king. He is all healed up and keeping himself busy with his hands and feet. The magic of Avalon does more than just heal him but keeping him young and at health. He is building a house at the southern part of the island where there are plenty of fish and games in the area. To find out more about my honor guest, I take on one of my human incarnations of an elderly woman named "Evelyn". When Evelyn approaches him, he gently greets her in his native tongue "Shalom." She recognizes, it is Hebrew. Evelyn returns the same gesture and follows by "Your Majesty" with respect to his lineage as loyalty. To his surprise, he turns away and chuckles with a little laughter. Curious and utterly dumbfounded, she asks him if she had said something funny or being disrespectful to him. After a moment in thought, He apologizes for his display of uncontrollable outbursts but appreciates for the much-needed laughter and levity. He shares with her about his sad and lonely journey filled with disappointment and human miseries that would cripple anyone from simple pleasure of such as cracking a smile or a laughter. When he finally calms down, he reveals to her that he is a king by divine right and not by noble birth. Thus, he is part celestial being and part human from a constellation of Pisces descending to earth to be born a celestial king and reigning over the age of Pisces. His reign is coming to an end, and he wants nothing more than to die a quick death. Nevertheless, the gods would not let him die, not until he produces an heir.

At the Eve of the age Aquarius, King Pisces must produce an heir soon. One that will usher humanity into the coming age of Aquarius which reigning for the next stretch of millennia. This is the reason that the gods keeping him here hidden away on Avalon. The gods assure him that they will gather as many concubines as needed to help him produces a powerful heir befitting the next celestial king. She also declares to him that she is Evelyn of Avalon here to assist him. Additionally, he possesses the mark of Avalon which makes him one of her children. Thus, she announces to him that in the future he shall be known as King Alpha, and Avalon is his home. Nevertheless, she must retire back to her slumber. With gratitude, he wishes her a rested sleep as she parts way to rejoin Avalon in her long sleep.

PRINCES and PRINCESSES

Who goes there? Who dares interrupting my sleep?

There are children running around laughing and being playful. Evelyn startles them with her sudden outburst of loud cry, "where is King Alpha?" The children are too frightened by her voice to stay around. Instead, they are running away and disappearing into the woods. The woods and vegetation are denser and thicker than before. *How long have I been asleep this time?* She ponders. Nevertheless, she is having a difficult time finding her way through the island. As Evelyn manages to make her way down to the southern part of the island, she is surprised to see a thriving village full of life with a field for farming and plantation. This is a well-established village. Slowly, she is approaching the village. A familiar face comes out to greet her. It is King Alpha.

"Welcome back, Grand Elder Evelyn." Said King Alpha.

"It is good to see you again King Alpha." Evelyn greeted him back. "You have been busy...."

King Alpha is happy and relief to see her. He informs her that she is been gone for at least seven years and apologizes for disturbing her. The children are keeping their distances and hiding behind the bushes that surrounding the village.

"Who are these people?" Evelyn asked.

"They are the children of Avalon." Said King Alpha." Some are mine, and the others are brought here by the gods. War is coming, and the children are not safe out there. They are being hunted by the churches. Many have died, and these are the survivors and your legacy."

King Alpha calls out to them to come closer and introduce themselves to their matriarch. Even so, they are reluctant to come any closer.

"Why are they still over there and not coming closer?" Evelyn asked. "Why are they not obeying you?"

"They are scared of you." Said King Alpha. "You are the only white person on this island, and many of the children here have never seen a white person before, or some may have had a bad experience with white people in the past. After all, they are being hunted by the churches, by white people."

"Dear God! I didn't know!" Evelyn cried out. "The poor things, they must be so terrified of me."

Evelyn spots a boulder near her and sits on it to rest her tired legs. She wastes no time and going ahead casting her songbird spell that will heal their souls and reduces the negative effects of trauma from their ordeals. The songbird has a hypnotic effect on the children, it relaxes them. The children are now drawn to Evelyn and her songbird. One by one they are approaching her and closing in on her. When the songbird comes to end, the children are already surrounded Evelyn. No longer frightened by Evelyn, the children see her as their mother. The youngest girl standing in front with arms reaching out to Evalyn, "Mama." Evelyn scoops her up and hold her tight. The other children are collapsing into Evelyn hugging and holding on to her. Such beautiful union, everyone lets out tears of joy and relief to have found Evelyn. Even the harden King Alpha drops down on his knees and let out good cry. It has been a long journey for everyone. However, a sound of a woman screaming in pain interrupts what it should have been a harmonious union of kindred souls. It is a sound from a woman in labor.

The woman in agonizing pain prompts Evelyn to turn her attention to King Alpha. He turns to her gaze.

"It must be one of the concubines," said King Alpha, "and she is heavily pregnant and due anytime now."

Without hesitation, Evelyn breaks off from the children and rushes behind King Alpha toward the house where the pregnant woman is staying in. A side from being a magical being, Evelyn is also an experienced midwife. She joins in with the other midwifes that are already there and delivers a healthy baby boy. After the ordeal, Evelyn calls out for King Alpha to come in and have a look at his proud creation. He gently cradles the newborn baby into his arms and cries.

"I am finally free." Said King Alpha. "This is my number eleven and final. He will be the Crown Prince Aquarius who will inherit my crown someday."

King Alpha calls out to his other children to join them and be presented to Evelyn.

"Behold great mother Evelyn." said King Alpha. "These are the princes and princesses of Avalon, born and raised here on the sacred ground of Avalon. Like me, they are all incarnated-celestial beings."

Unaware to everyone, the daylight situation is changing drastically. The day is turning into night. In an instance, the mysterious darkness engulfs the entire island. Everyone is scared and starts panicking. With a flick of her fingers, Evelyn magically summons dozens of orbs of white light that hovering in midair and illuminate the entire house. Evelyn is doing her best trying to calm everyone by reminding them that they are in Avalon, and no one will be in any real danger. Avalon protects all her children. Just when things returning to normal, a column of white light from above pierces through the dark cloud and lights up the surrounding as bright as the sun. The mysterious darkness is gradually vanishing and turning back into a daylight. Jubilation returns to everyone smile and laughter. However, Evelyn perceives it as omen of the things to come. Thus, she interrupts the cheery moment with a loud, sinister laugh.

"In all my years," said Evelyn, "I have never felt such power. So unbridled and destructive, this child can destroy worlds many times over and remaking it just as many. He is both, dark and light. He commands light and dark. Oh…King Alpha, you have outdone yourself with this one. The age of Aquarius will be the age of many great wonders and destructions the likes of which have not been seen since the age of the gods."

Everyone is stunned by her revelation. King Alpha cannot help but feeling perplexed and ambivalent upon knowing of what will happen in the coming age. Nevertheless, Evelyn assures everyone that they are perfectly safe here and protected by the magic of Avalon.

"Absolutely no human or demon on Avalon." Said Evelyn. "Only divine and magical beings are allowed to be here."

Evalyn continues with her balancing act of trying to get everyone to remain calm. Doing so, she insinuates herself into their lives and assumes the role as their matriarch.

"From now on," said Evelyn, "you are all my children. As your mother, I will love and protect all of you with all my divine powers. I will teach you how to use the magic of this world and share with you the knowledge of the ancient."

Within days, most of the children are now flocked around Evelyn like baby chicks with mother hen. When they are hungry, they eat. When they are tired, they sleep, and always with Evelyn. As for the grownups, they have many tasks assigned to them daily. Some are helping King Alpha tending the crops and livestock, and others are helping Evelyn with the children. But in their spare times, they are being guided and tutored in ways of using their magics by Evelyn. However, King Alpha will take no part in it. He rather be left alone tending to the crops and the livestock. Nevertheless, Evelyn enjoys her new role very much that she does not have the need to go back to Avalon. Thus, she remains both a mother and a teacher to the children day and night.

THE TEACHINGS OF "EVELYN"

THE ISLAND OF FIRST MAN (ADAM)

All human beings are the descendants of Adam, the first man. Not from the children of Adam and Eve, but an archetype or principle of how human genetic makeup in our core beings are being made, of earth or of matters. Such that, inside every matter contains two opposite forces of positive and negative. Likewise, inside every human being contains two opposite forces of good and evil. Supposedly, Adam betrays God by consuming the forbidden fruit from the tree of the knowledge of good and evil. For such rebellious act, Adam is casted out from paradise and disposed onto Earth for eternity. The body of Adam is now lying asleep as an island of Angkor Wat in Cambodia. The five temples on the island are the trees of the knowledge of good and evil. The big temple in the middle is the tree of the knowledge of evil, and the other four surrounding temples are the trees of the knowledge of good. The four surrounding trees are the only container for preventing the knowledge of evil from corrupting the world.

The fruit from the tree of the knowledge of good and evil contains billions of seeds. When consumes by an unsuspecting host, the seeds will latch onto the soul of the host taking over the host body like parasite. The parasitic seeds take roots and grow out from the body of the host and into three trees, one being the tree of the knowledge of evil and the other two being the trees of the knowledge of good.

MAN (OR DEMON)

To this day, the parasitic seeds continue to grow and prosper in every human being of this dimension of earth. From a young-soul reincarnation, human would enjoy the illusions of so call destiny that the seeds have mapped out for them. All experiences whether physical or emotional will be fed into the invisible trees of the knowledge of good and evil. However, should the host body die, the trees will move on with the soul to the next reincarnation body and repeating the cycle over again. Until such time, the trees are coming to maturation. Thus, the demons from the abyss will come up to feed on them by devouring the souls with the fully grown trees. If the soul is not harvested by demon in time, the trees will pollute the soul with their evil and turning the host body into demon, into cannibalism, serial killer, serial rapist, pedophile, psychopath etc. Should demon numbers on the rise, the universe will resort to the cleansing of the world, again.

THE FOUR-GREAT CLEANSINGS OF WORLDS

Like Adam, human will find a way to rebel against God. Each time this happens, God ends up setting destruction to the entire world. The first is destruction by winds. The second is destruction by fire. The third is destruction by ice. And the last but not the least, is destruction by water, the great flood.

After the great flood, the gods conclude their findings. From where they stand, they will continue destroying humans indefinitely until some drastic measures must be introduced to the human equations. However, humans by themselves are incapable of finding way to rid themselves from the trees of the knowledge of good and evil; they cannot purge themselves from the cursed trees. Infect, they develop a dependency with the trees, and knowing that they will turn demons or become demon fodders themselves. Thus, the gods introduce some highly evolved souls of their own to the human collectives to guide human away from the influence of the trees and back to God.

These highly evolved souls are collected from the vastness of all creations. Some travels the great distances to get here from the other side of the universe. Others are from different time and space or even from another universe. All are here with the same prime directive to guide the lost souls back to God.

THE THREE GREAT AGES

THE AGE BEFORE, NOW, AND BEYOND

THE AGE OF PISCES, AQUARIUS, CAPRICORN, AND NOTHING

12	11	10	0
3	2	1	0

THE GREAT AGES

To begin any Age, a great sacrifice must be made to appease the world demons. The divine must make this offering from some of their own flesh and blood for the Age of Pisces. Henceforth, sacrificing for the Age of Aquarius demands all the beloved children of a goddess. The great Ages are the measures of the lifespans of the trees of the knowledge of good and evil in humans. Every Age begins when the trees are starting to grow and ends when the trees reaching maturation roughly 2,500+ years. This is somewhat true with the passing of Age of Pisces. However, no one Age is the same as the next. Every Age is different according to the growth of the trees of that Age. Some are longer than others. Thus, we are living in the Age of high literacy rate and having every information predisposed to us in the palm of our hands. This bombardment of information makes or accelerates the growth of the trees and resulting in the trees maturing faster rate. Provided that there is no cataclysmic event pending, then the Age of Aquarius will surely be shorter than the Age of Pisces.

THE AGE OF PISCES, THE AGE BEFORE

1 - 2

Pisces is significant with number 12 being the zodiac sign of number twelve in astrology. The Age of Pisces begins with the sacrifices of many children of the gods. Under the influence of the Age of Pisces, 12 is comprised in all things of great significant: there are twelve zodiac signs in astrology, 12 months in a year, 12 hours in a day, 12 inches in a foot, 12 Olympian Gods, 12 apostles, and etcetera.

12, THE AGE OF INEQUALITY

With 12 dominating all aspects of our lives, the Age of Pisces is consisted of number 1 not being equal to 2. This denotes inequality in all things under the Age of Pisces. This is the Age of masters and slaves. This is the Age of kings, of dictators, of generals, of warlords and so on... At work or other employment, the boss is the law and in charged. Right or wrong, the boss is always right. At home, the husband is always the boss and king.

12, OPPOSITES ATTRACT

With number 1 not being equal 2, the opposite is true that man will always attracts to women. In a relationship, it is always consisted of a man and a woman. However, the inequality of number 12 extends even beyond love. It creates an imbalance in a relationship. Thus, the Age of Pisces spreads infidelity, polygamy, and other illicit affairs....

THE AGE OF AQUARIUS, The AGE OF NOW

1 = 1

Aquarius is significant with number 11 being the zodiac sign of number eleven in astrology. The Age of Aquarius begins when the churches burn all the children of a goddess in the late-eighteen century, England. Under the influent of the Age of Aquarius, 11 is comprised in all things of great significant....

11, THE AGE OF EQUALITY AND FAIRNESS

With 11 dominating all aspects of our lives, the Age of Aquarius is consisted of number 1 being equal and identical to the other number 1. This symmetry of number 11 denotes equality and fairness in all things under the Age of Aquarius. This is the Age of gender equality; this is the age of fairness. Those kings and those pigs that we are called bosses, they have no real powers and no real authorities over us. In fact, they are just puppets or figureheads for us to use. We are the real power, and we are all mattered.

11, LIKE ATTRACTS LIKE

With number 1 being equal to another number 1, man will only attract to a woman of the same interest and similarity and vice versa. This is the Age of soulmates and true loves. If it is not true, then it will not be love. However true, the symmetry in attractions will also prompt the rise of the same sex marriages of all genders. No longer a husband nor a wife, but an equal partner in family and in love.

A PROPHECY FOR THE AGE of AQUARIUS

With fairness and equality, the Age of Aquarius will be blessed by the Divines. At the height of the Age of Aquarius, a Goddess of innocent will be born into the world. With her come the blessings of love and prosperity.

THE GREAT COUNTDOWN

3 – 2 – 1 – 0

The great countdown for humanity starts from the Age of Pisces and ends with the Age of Capricorn. The Age of Pisces is number 12, or 3. Succeeding that is the Age of Aquarius and with a number 11, or 2. Lastly, humanity ends with the Age of Capricorn and number 10, or 1. The great clock of humanity is counting down from 3, 2, and 1. After the Age of Capricorn, the great humanity will cease to be.

THE AGE OF CAPRICORN, THE AGE BEFORE THE END

1 – 0

Capricorn is significant with number 10 being the zodiac sign of number ten in astrology. The Age of Capricorn will begin with the sacrifice from the divines to bring forth the Age before THE END. With 10 or 1 dominating all our lives, the Age of Capricorn represents the pinnacle of man in both intellect and spirituality. Half of the world populations are already uploaded their consciousnesses into an advanced-virtual heaven. There, they can exist indefinitely. The others are downloaded their consciousnesses into artificial bodies or into series of clones. Asexuality or lack thereof is the trend of the Age. However, some find loves through artificial means of sexual companionships from robots or androids. There is no government. The world is run and managed by a singular-godlike-artificial intelligent….

LESSONS END

PART II

BACK TO AVALON

Ten years have passed since the birth of Prince Aquarius. Being the youngest, Prince Aquarius is always being spoiled and overprotected by others. They never let him out from their sights. After all, he is the Crown Prince who will inherit the crown from King Alpha. The other children are all grown up into their teens and capable of performing magic on their own... The adults are also grown proficient with most of Evelyn's teachings. Some are helping and assisting Evelyn in mentoring the teens. This gives Evelyn more freedom to pursue her other matters. Evelyn needs to know what is happening out there in the world of man and how many children of Avalon are still alive. She needs to find and rescue the surviving children before is too late. Not in so many words, Evelyn lets everyone know that she is going somewhere out there doing something important and will be awhile for her return. After assigning tasks to the adults, she is off on her journey.

In the absence of Evelyn, everyone is more open and casual than before. Such that, they are all seemed to be curious about the same thing, "why is there not a single white people on the island?" No one has the clear answer. However, they try asking King Alpha and only to be met with disappointment. Finally, they are all agreed that Evelyn is the only person who can shed light on things. No one will dare asking her the question, at least not directly.

MANIDA

Within months before Prince Aquarius 15th birthday and his rite of passage to be crowned King, Evelyn makes her return from her long and arduous journey. Trailing behind her is a small group of survivors seeking sanctuary on Avalon. The youngest among the newcomers is Manida. She is the first survivor that Evelyn rescues on her journey. Manida is from Laos, a landlock country in Southeast Asia. Although Manida is now fifteen-year-old girl, she spends years travelling the world and learning magic under Evelyn. Everyone is taking a liking to her and drawn to her warm and beautiful smile especially Prince Aquarius. The connection between two is instantaneous. The two are becoming closer each passing day until they become inseparable. Thus, Evelyn is taking notice and coming to her conclusion with a realization that these two beautiful souls have finally found each other. Evelyn sees this moment of great potential and take the opportunity to deliver her invocation of ancient rite.

"Come," said Evelyn, "my two beautiful treasures. Prince Aquarius, your heart is pure as gold, and someday you will be King. No matter who you are in your next life, may your reign over the humanity be just and fair. There will be many trials and tribulations. But should you falter and fall, Manida will be there to catch you and mends your broken soul. She is your destiny and your soul companion, and she is hard and sharp as diamond. Together, the two of you will always be happy and complete. May the sacred star of Avalon guides and protects the two of you, always."

MANIDA AND HER DILEMMA

As newcomer to the island, Manida is full of curiosities and adventures. This is not always a good thing for her. Shortly after her arrival to the island, she starts asking everyone a question about why there are no other white people on the island. With exception to Evelyn for being white, there is no other white people. However, no one can give her a straight answer, not even Prince Aquarius. Some are completely ignoring the question and be on their ways. This goes on incessantly for many days and until one day. One of the adults comes up with a solution to appease everyone curiosity, especially Manida. This curious adult instructs Manida to approach Evelyn for the truth about the matter. Manida agrees that the only person can help her is Evelyn.

Wasting little time, Manida approaches Evelyn. To everyone surprise, she asks the question.

"Great Mother," asked Manida, "why isn't there any other White people on the island other than yourself?"

This usually soft-spoken girl speaks at great volume and catches everyone's attention. No one dares move; everyone is staying still and poised motionless. The reluctant Evelyn turns her head and looks on pensively thinking in her deep thought. Manida continues expressing more of her rantings.

"We are living on an island surrounded by white people." Said Manida. "On our way here, we were passing through towns after towns full of white people. Yet, there is not a single white people here but you. Why?"

The long silence finally comes to an end when Evelyn delivers her revelation. She takes in a deep breath and slowly exhaling then turning back facing her beloved Manida.

"My dear child," said Evelyn, "and everyone here, the answer that you are looking for will not set you free instead it will only burden you even more… The reason is white people are the ones leading the rebellion against the gods right now. I know that humans are inherently evil, but white people are something else. This I am certain because I am white just like them. In these pass three hundred years, they have committed genocides across the continents and killed most of my children and my friends; they have tried to destroy the temples of the gods. That made the gods angry, and they will never make white children for me, ever. You are what remained the only children of Avalon."

Evelyn ends the lesson early in the day and instructs everyone to take the opportunity to work on their own tasks during their time off. She needs to be left alone for the day.

The reactions among the children and the adults are mixed in their feelings and emotions. Some are more perplexed than others. However, Manida does not believed that all white people are bad. She thinks that everyone comes to love and respect Evelyn as mother and as teacher who also happens to be white. Thus, Manida hopes that everyone will come to this mutual understanding on their own terms.

RISE THE PHOENIX

Everyone is learning and adapting well to Evelyn teachings. Some are more proficient than others. However, most are developed into their own gifts and techniques. Up until now, only the adults are allowed when it comes to the more complexed and advanced magics such as self-transformation or shapeshifting. Manida, on the other hand, is in no hurry for the advanced stuffs. Although she is gifted with a powerful precognitive ability, Manida just wants to be a kid and enjoy herself with Prince Aquarius. She is not alone. The other children and even some of the adults are wanting the same thing to be closed to Prince Aquarius. Thus, Manida senses a minor tension and even jealousy from the others whenever she is around Prince Aquarius. As new arrival to the island, Manida is unaware of the true depth to Prince Aquarius powers, and she will soon find out.

On this day with a clear-blue sky, Prince Aquarius is accompanied by Manida going off somewhere for a special occasion. He wants to do something extraordinary with his power, and he needs Manida to see who he is in his pure form after the transformation. For the first time in his life, Prince Aquarius will attempt shapeshifting. A task so privy that only the adults are allowed. However, today is Prince Aquarius day and he will have his turn.

Finally, they are far enough from any prying eyes. Prince Aquarius instructs Manida to wait for him in a safe distance out in an open field while he will stay hidden deep in the woods. There, he will summon his power to perform his metamorphosis and changing into the ultimate state of his physical being. No matter what happen, Manida cannot interfere.

Suddenly, the whole island is turning into night by a mysterious darkness. Gradually, the dark mist is gathering itself and becoming concentrated in one spot right where Prince Aquarius is. He is summoning his dark power which necessary to complete his transformation. However, Manida is keeping her distance and helpless to do anything but a frightened witness to a phenomenon unknown to her. Although the strange-dark mist is dissipating from the island, a new powerful presence is manifesting. Its psychic-auric field is inundating those with a psychic sensitivity. Manida is incapacitated and unable to move. Then, everything is suddenly stopped, and the surrounding noises are dead silenced. This eerily silence lasts, and it is being interrupted by a colossal movement of something big. The powerful presence is now moving and heading out from the woods making its way toward Manida.

The naive and petrified Manida can only stand and watch while the beast is plowing down everything in its path. It is coming toward her. However, Manida could not clearly make out what it is that she is looking at. Despite the obvious colossal presence, Manida cannot see any discernible body but only movement in vegetations. Not only this thing is big, but it is also invisible. Finally, it makes its way out from the woods. The beast ceases its movement and materializes itself right in front of Manida. To her astonishment, Manida is watching the great beast materializing into a giant bird, or a giant eagle.

Enraptured by the displays of the awesome power of the beast, Manida falls to knees in reverence to the presence of great power and majesty from the beast. She struggles to stay conscious and keeping herself from passing out. However, the beast is realizing that its proximity to her is putting her in danger. The beast must keep its distance from her. Before the beast takes off, it tries to communicate with her through telepathic link to comfort her.

"Little one, it's me." Said the Beast. "I am Prince Aquarius. I am sorry. But do not be afraid, and everything is going to be all right. I must go now."

The beast takes a few hops and stretches out its great wings. With a single push from its powerful legs, it leaps into the air and becomes airborne soaring upward high toward the blue sky. When it reaches its intended height, the beast adjusts angle of flight path and glides ever so effortlessly over the island. Then, it lets out a loud cry. Shrieking and echoing like thunders, the sound travels far and can be heard miles away in all directions. Upon hearing the loud cry, everyone on the island is looking upward toward the sky fixating on the great beast in wonders.

The presence of the beast surprises Evelyn. Gradually, the situation becomes clear to her that the huge presence earlier is none other than Prince Aquarius himself. Nevertheless, she gazes upon the beast with great wonders and allowing herself adrift in her thought, *wow, he has finally done it. The great Phoenix has awoken and making himself known to world.* Now she needs to let everyone know and making sure that everything is ok.

"My children," said Evelyn. "Stay calm my children… That is none other than Prince Aquarius himself. He has taken his beast form to show the world that king of the new age has arrived. Behold my children, the great Phoenix has graced himself to us with his divine presence and may his blessings bestow upon us all."

The beast is flying in circle around the island before heading off toward the western sky. This extraordinary event electrifies everyone to become more studious than before in their pursuit of magic. However, Manida is the only one who is in no mood to celebrate for the moment. As always, Evelyn can sense something troubling with Manida and it is something to do with Prince Aquarius. Instead, Evelyn exercises caution not to let Manida burden herself any longer.

"My dear child," said Evelyn, "do not worry yourself too much. Prince Aquarius will soon be king of the new age. His power is beyond any of us to comprehend. No one is going to stop him from anything... He can do whatever he wants. Do not worry yourself and just let him be. When he is tired of flying around, he will come right back to you."

That brings Manida some comfort for the moment. The following day, Prince Aquarius is back with his human form intact and rushing toward Manida. The two souls are more than happy to be reunited again. The tired Prince is more concerned about Manida than anything else. Nevertheless, the Prince succumbs to fatigue and exhaustion due to the nature of his ordeal. Thus, he slowly crouches down to his knees and collapses to the ground falling into deep sleep next to Manida.

THE NEW CELESTIAL KING

The long-awaited birthday is finally here. Everyone is participating in the ceremony because today is Prince Aquarius turn to be crowned king. However, the greater island is home to many others magical beings that reside on Avalon long before the arrival of the children. Many of these beings will also be making their appearances to witness the crowning of the new king. Most of the humanoid participants are at their best in their late Victorian era. Amazingly, King Alpha surprises everyone by showing up wearing a crown on his head.

The sacred crown on top of his head is stirring up some commotions among the gatherings. King Alpha must come up with something quickly before the situation is getting out of hand. To pacify this situation, King Alpha explains that the sacred crown only appears once the new king is chosen. Such, it would magically appear in one day during the sun rise in the morning on the head of the current king. The appearance of the crown only last until high noon of the same day, then it would disappear again. No one touches the sacred crown, and only the chosen Kings are allowed.

The tired King Alpha approaches the gathering where Prince Aquarius sits in the middle awaiting to be crowned as the next Celestial King. The prince is seated on a simple chair facing south and surrounded by the gatherings. However, Evelyn and Manida are standing nearby and unable to have any contact with neither the prince nor the King. The reign of the Celestial King is an absolute and a solitary one; his is a power that cannot be shared nor be equaled by anyone. Thus, there is no queen for the Celestial King.

With haste, King Alpha takes his ceremonial position by standing behind the sitting prince. With both hands, the King lifts the sacred crown off from his head and holding it just above the head of the prince. The following is the King sharing his speech of affirmation and emotional good-bye.

"There are two events in my long life that I am truly happy." Said King Alpha. "The day I was crowned king and the other is today. With this sacred crown, you will be king. Therefore, you will inherit all my powers and my wisdoms. This will make you the king, and I will cease to be."

The King gently places the crown on the head of the prince and delivers his final speech.

"You are now King Aquarius." Said King Alpha.

Instantly, King Alpha dematerializes into nothing. He is gone.....

The sudden disappearance of the former King shocks everyone. Up until now, no one really knows how the process supposed to work except for the late King Alpha. One by one, the participants are lining up to pay a respect to the newly crowned King Aquarius. However, many are still wailing from the shock of losing their beloved King. The new King is giving his first speech in a form of solace to alleviate some of the emotional pains from losing someone very dear.

"His body maybe gone," said King Aquarius, "but his essence lives in me now. I inherit some of his memories and his wisdoms. His magic was keeping him alive until today. He regrets not letting anyone knows about the process and how it ends. Nevertheless, he was happy."

The bewildered gathering is gradually dispersing and going back to their daily routines. However, the other magical beings are also disappearing back to their perspective dwellings. The two that are staying behind are Evelyn and Manida. They want to witness the disappearance of the crown and keeping the new King companied. The new King must remain seated until the crown disappears, and for fear that he might accidently having a physical contact with others.

A high noon at last, the new King can relax from the burden of having to wear the sacred crown. The crown is starting to fade away from his head until there is nothing left of it. After the disappearance of the crown, the new King hobs from his chair and runs to Manida to celebrate his successful transfer of power from a prince to a King. However, the celebration is short lived. Monida falls to the ground and overwhelmed by the ominous-psychic visions of burning, of fire.

THE OMINOUS VISION

Everyone on the island is plagued by this vision on some levels. However, the intensity is more severe among the gifted ones like Manida. The dreadful sounds of fear coming from the others are seriously disturbing and disrupting this otherwise a tranquil sanctuary. This makes Evelyn uneasy, and she is not immune to anything that poses a threat to her beloved children. The ominous vision does not linger around long. It too gradually fades away, and it leaves behind many traumatized children of whom are being tended to by Evelyn. For the first time in her life, Evelyn is feeling helpless and uncertain. Without King

Alpha by her side, she is now alone facing the inevitable or maybe the end....

The vision maybe gone but, the remains are disturbing memories of what will happen in the future to come. To understand better, Evelyn asks Manida to go over into more details about the horrible vision portending the calamity that is to come.

"The fire is everywhere." Explained Manida. "The churches found us, and we are surrounded. They lock all of us in the main house and pile some woods over while we are still trapped inside. Thus, they burn us alive, and we all die."

"We all die" is the last thing Evelyn wants to hear and the very thing that sets her off. No matter what happens, Evelyn must remain calm so the children will not lose fate in her. She needs to seek counsel from the gods and hoping to hear the truth from their deliverance. Before that, she needs to keep the children from losing fate in her and that Avalon is still safe and protected from demons and humans. Meanwhile, Evelyn is trying to put all her affairs in order. After gaining back some trusts from her beloved children, she instructs all the adults to carry on with their assigned tasks while she is gone. It will be sometimes until her return.

Evelyn does not resort to lie or hide things from the children. For their sake, she does it to protect them. The truth is Evelyn had already tried to contact the gods. However, no one responds to her. This is very unusual for the gods to remain silenced even to the distressed call from the matriarch of Avalon. She suspects something is wrong and wants to find out for herself. She needs to go to the place where the gods live; she needs to go far east to the land with the mountain so high that it can reach heaven.

THE REVELATION OF THE GODS

Evelyn hates a long good-bye, and off she goes heading toward the highest mountain on earth. There, she will meet with the gods. The home of the gods is on the edge of the world between heaven and earth. However, the journey there is long and may provide just enough time for her to come up with a contingency plan should things go sideways with the gods. She is aware that the ominous vision from the gods is absolute and fears the gods might have gone back on their words. Although, that possibility exists, and there is still time for her to convince them from going through with it. If all else failed with the gods, Evelyn may consider doing something unpredictable to get even with both the gods and the churches. As a last resort, Evelyn might consider doing something evil....

The relentless Evelyn is now reaching Nepal a country near the base of the highest mountain. With little time, she is making her final preparation to meet with the gods. As a skilled shapeshifter, Evelyn assumes a form that is suitable for a harsh climate condition such as something big and hairy. Traversing the highest mountain on earth is no small task, but she endures the elements and reaches the top in good time. There, the gods are expecting and welcoming her through an opening portal leading her to the home of the gods.

All pleasantries aside, Evelyn begins her petitioning and implores the gods to have mercy with her children.

"You must know why I am here." Said Evelyn. "Why are my children being condemned to such a cruel fate? What are their crimes? What evil have they done to deserve this?"

Reluctantly, they respond.

"The children are innocence." Said the gods." They have committed no crimes. Regrettably, we want you to know that it is for the greater good. Their sacrifices will save many innocence lives. The world demons will stop controlling the churches, and the killing of the innocence will cease. We have great plan for churches. Under our guidance, the churches will become the new guiding lights to many that seek our salvations."

Before Evelyn can have any saying, a white light flashes and blinds her temporary. When Evelyn opens her eyes again, she is surprised to find herself back at the base of the mountain. The gods transport her out from their home, and she is no longer welcome there. Evelyn feels betrayed by the gods and suspecting them of working in collusion with the churches. Also, Evelyn is experiencing an awakening that in this world there is no right or wrong, and there is no good or evil. Just like the gods,

Evelyn wants to do something right and for the greater good of her children. However, she wants to make both the gods and the churches to pay for what they are about to do with her children. As it stands, Evelyn is no match for them. Going up against the gods, she is going to need more than just her anger. Evelyn needs an army, an army of darkness.

THE ROOT OF HELL

Before heading back to Avalon, Evelyn needs to make a detour to collect something. Part goddess and part witch, Evelyn is familiar with myriad forms of dark arts and forbidden magics. Hidden away at the gate of Hell is the staff of a forbidden magic. She needs it to complete part of her plan. The staff is part of Evelyn long and forgotten history. However, the staff is too dangerous to be left in this world unguarded. The gate of Hell seems to be a perfect place to hide it. Although the journey to Hell is done many times in the past for Evelyn to recue souls that are mistakenly taken, this time is different. This time she needs something from hell, something that will augment her power so great it will rival that of the gods; she needs the root of Hell.

Upon her arrival to the gate of Hell, Evelyn seems to be hesitating and recollecting her past services to the gods. Whatever is asked of her and no matter how challenging the task, she always fulfills her part. Now, she feels that they betray her and consign her precious children to the murderous hands of the churches. That, she demands justice. However, there will be no justice for her today or ever. As a goddess, she feels that it is within her rights to bring justice to the gods and the churches. Thus, she will deliver her own justice. If the light should sway from its path, then it shall be corrected by the dark.

Without further hesitation, Evelyn enters the gate of Hell.

VANISHING AVALON

Life on Avalon is far from back to being normal. With King Alpha gone and the where about of Evelyn is unclear, the situation on Avalon is looking somewhat dim. Manida and the others are still plagued by the visions of The End, regardless. Most of the adults are starting to lose faith in themselves, and hopelessness is spreading and everywhere. However, everyone is still hanging on to a firm belief that it is safe here on Avalon. All they can do now is waited for the return of their Matriarch and with hopes of something good to this. Nevertheless, it has been over a month since the parting of Evelyn. She is supposed to be back days ago. The adults are uncertain about when she will return, and if that were still a possibility. They are considering of waiting it out a little longer before abandoning the sanctuary and venture out from the safety of Avalon. They plan to follow Evelyn to India and hope to blend in better with the indigenous people. It is risky, but it is better than just waiting here only to die. They do not have to wait long. Throughout the village, peoples are suddenly shouting and jumping with joys. Evelyn is back.

Like a mother misses her child, Evelyn is going around with hugs and kisses to all her children. Afterward, she calls out to everyone to come closer and hear of what she learns from the gods. She informs everyone that the vision is true. However, it may come to pass if she uses the staff given by the gods to specifically remove dark manas from the children. Evelyn claims that the churches fear the children because of their dark manas. If they discovered that the children are no longer possessed dark manas, then they might show mercy. Evelyn is convincing and genuine that the children are too eagerly trusting her. Unaware of Evelyn ulterior motive, they want nothing to do with their dark manas anymore. Thus, they want them gone.

One by one, Evelyn uses the staff on the children. The staff is about five-foot long and eerily dark with two prongs at the end of its tip. It shapes like a fork used for hay making by farmer of the time. Evelyn would jap the tips at the children. The staff instantly sucks out and drains the dark manas when used. However, Evelyn claims that the dark manas flow through her and into the ground. It is another lie. The dark manas flow out from the children and directly into the body of Evelyn. She is secretly collecting all the dark manas to herself. Within hour, she is finished with all the children, but the young King Aquarius is the last.

The process of hoarding this large amount of dark manas into her body is taking a toll on Evelyn. She is suffering from fatigue and exhaustion. Everyone is urging her to stop and rest for a while until she feels better. However, Evelyn is determined and would not stop. She keeps pressing on to her last target; she keeps pressing on to King Aquarius. During the process of taking on King Aquarius, Evelyn collapses and unconscious. She never finishes. Leaving only King Aquarius who is left with the dark manas.

With great concern, the children put their Matriarch to her rest. She is not to go near the staff nor perform anymore act. Evelyn sleeps through out the day and into the night. However, the children are unaware that Evelyn soul is being devoured by the immense-dark manas from within her. She is literally being transformed into an abomination, into a demon. The old Evelyn is no more….

"The island is gone." Said Manida. "Avalon is gone…."

DARK EVELYN

The day that everyone fears is here; the day that Avalon disappears is finally happened. The children are waking up this morning to find that they are no longer on Avalon, although the livestock and the village are still there. The adults are frantically rushing to the outer edge of the village to find nothing and not a trace of Avalon. Confused and afraid, the children are turning their attentions to Evelyn, the only person who can shed light on this. However, Evelyn is nowhere to be found. She is not in her sleeping quarter. The children call out her name, and some are shouting everywhere for her. Nevertheless, no response from her. Finally, someone locates her eating in the kitchen. Thus, they approach her and shout her name. She appears unresponsive to their calls, then someone grabs her and calls her "Evelyn".

The children are oblivious to the sudden disappearance of Avalon, and the metamorphosis happening inside the body of Evelyn. The internal change is morphing Evelyn into something else, a demon. However, the two events are connected. The moment Evelyn turns, instantly, it causes Avalon to vanish. There can never be a human nor a demon presence on Avalon. Fate is not without an irony as she attempts to harness the dark manas fails and backfires her which forever changing her into a demon. A newly awaken demon, Evelyn must learn to suppress her demonic desires in the presence of the children fearing that they might learn about her true nature. Demon or not, Evelyn will always love her children.

Khamsone Limsavanh

FOOD FOR DEMON

Now a demon, Evelyn does not have a compunction with lying. She is telling everyone that she overslept during the night and now very hungry. This causes her to get up in morning and bakes some pies. As always, Evelyn askes some of the children to join her. Most of the children are too eager to have a meal with their beloved Matriarch. Thus, they join in and partake the meal which is prepared diligently by Evelyn. The instant they bite into it, they become ill. Terrified and quilt-stricken, Evelyn cries out for help.

Wasting little time, Evelyn confesses in front of everyone.

"This is my fault." Said Evelyn. "I did this to myself and to my children. I want to control the dark manas that I have absorbed and use it against the gods. Instead, it turns me into this, a demon. I am no longer welcome in the light of the Creator and Avalon. I am responsible for the disappearance of Avalon and the impending demises to all of you. I have been out at night hunting nearby human town for human babies to satisfy my hunger. I am still evolving as demon and will continue to evolve perhaps into a true demon. I am sorry, but this is the path I have chosen."

On the request by Evelyn, the adults move her to a place of isolation and far away from the village. A powerful spell is placed around the village to keep Evclyn and other dark entities from entering. However, demons are the least of their problems.

Humans are being spotted nearby. They have been tracking on the trail left behind by Evelyn, and it is leading the humans back to the village. Before nightfall, the village is being surrounded. The humans encircle the village with armed sentries and series of small campfires. By morning, the main forces have arrived and formed a small army. Thus, they begin their approaches into the village.

BURN, HEATHEN BURN

The army equipped with their Victorian era weapons round off all the villagers which mostly consisted of non-white women and children, then place them in the center of the village. After they conclude their findings, they call the villagers "heathen" and quickly herd all of them into the main house. There, they block off all the doors and windows with piles of woods and continue piling more woods over the main house. In the mist of the mayhem, someone sets the main house on fire with all the women and the children still trapped inside. The men are behaving strangely as if they were in a trance. They are standing around the burning house and chanting repeatedly, "BURN, HEATHEN BURN." The chanting becomes so loud that they can no longer hear the screaming of the women and the children that are being burned alive. After they are tired of chanting, they continue burning the rest of the village.

GRIEVING EVELYN CURSED

The burnings are raging on throughout the day and into the night. By midnight, the great burnings are dying down to smoldering charcoals glowing like giant clusters of ambers and illuminated the night sky at the very heart of England. When looking down from above, one can plainly see a giant-dark portal is opening and unleashing dark-mysterious forces onto the world. Realizing that they have made a grave mistake, the gods unleash a rogue tornado touching it down on the burning site and scoops away all traces until nothing remains but a dark scar on the landscape. However, the efforts are in vain and too little, too late.

At the sight of a giant tornado on top them, the men flee the area in terror and fear that God have forsaken them. When things are settling down, the eerily silence permeates the dark landscape and the surrounding woods. A lone-falling star is streaking over the landscape and disappearing into the night sky. Heaven sheds its tear for the lost of its creation. A sign of a great calamity is descending on all mankind. War is coming.

In the middle of the dark landscape, a lonely shadowy figure appears. It is Evelyn. Her transformation is completed. Now, she is pure demon with dominion over all darkness. However, she weeps over the lost of her beloved children. Her wailing cry fills the dark-empty landscape. She wants the gods and the churches to be held accountable for the act of committing genocide of her children and her people. Thus, a curse is placed onto the world by Evelyn. With her dark army, she wants to wage war on the gods and destroys all humanity.

CHAPTER III

WAR

I am pandemonium; I am chaos; I AM WAR.

Among my kind, I am the lowest and the bottom feeder. On earth, however, I am revered a king, an emperor, and a god. Their ignorance empowers me, and their stupidities fuel my flame. Thus, I will scorch this earth for all eternity.

TWILIGHT OF MAN

A dawn of the 19th century is a dawn of the first great war, World War I. For the first time in modern history, the world is at war, a promise by Her-Dark-Majesty Evelyn. With her dark army, she instigates a catalyst by manipulating the already depraved men into slaughtering their friends and neighbors. The onslaught of killings is going back and forth to no end. However, the world is in no short supply of imbeciles and depraved men of whom will continue the killings. Thus, war is inevitable.

After the first World War, another World War awaits, and another and so forth. Until all humanity becomes extinct, only then the war will come to an end. However, the war between good and evil is just begun. A well-designed plan engineers by Dark-Evelyn herself. As she once stood by to watch her children perished, Evelyn wants to spare the Vatican Palace so they can watch their children murdering themselves around them while all Europe are burnt up in flame. Nevertheless, the gods in heaven also are at war with the army of darkness. It seems that the fate of mankind is heading toward the eventual destruction of itself.

HOPE 1.1

The gods are in panic mode scrambling all over cosmos in search of a weapon that they hope it would stop the army of darkness and end the wars. However, the gods found such weapon through their own long and forgotten history that they are once at war among themselves. During the age of the gods, the weapons are used and to great success. This weapon harnesses the power of the universe and destroys everything in its path. Nevertheless, the gods name such a weapon, "Angel of Destruction" (or a thermal nuclear weapon).

Without further delay, the knowledge of the weapon is disseminated into the chosen humans on earth provided with the guidance of how to build it. Within months, the humans are succeeded in building the first prototype atomic bomb. The test results are exceeding the expectation of the gods and a show of force as warning to the army of darkness. Thus, the atomic bomb is made possible as the result of a divine intervention.

The gods manipulate the human into using such weapon to obliterate the already evil-infested regions. The results are devastating. The explosions and chain reactions decimate everything in its blast radius. However, the weapon does not make a distinction. It simply destroys all, innocent and combatant alike. Those survived near the proximity of the blast will inevitably suffer long and agonizing deaths from severe exposure to radiation burns and radiation sicknesses. The gods are horrified by their own makings. The demons, however, welcome this new destructive power and only to hasten the destruction of mankind, more nuclear bombs please.

HOPE 1.2

Once again, the gods are in panic and rushing all over the world performing damage controls. The weapon works effectively during the age of the gods but fails against the demonic-infested humans. This causes the gods to second guess themselves and their inability to make the right decision. However, the gods enlist the help from the other worlds beyond the stars. The beings from the other worlds are invited here to stop the humans from destroying themselves with nuclear bombs.

The beings from other worlds are here and doing their parts to keep the humans from destroying themselves. However, the gods need to do more to ensure the survival of humanity. They begin to think outside the box and consider all options. The answer is staring in their faces all along. The gods need to bring back the children of Avalon. Thus, the children are being reincarnated back to life.

The early 1960's is the new dawn and the new beginning of hope for all humanity. The gods are beginning to bring back the children of Avalon. To ensure the safety and the wellbeing of the children, The gods hide their sacred markings and bound their powers. With the memories of their previous lives wiped clean, the children remember nothing of their pasts. One after another, the children are being inserted into many of the unsuspecting families throughout the world.

The sudden appearances of the children cause Evelyn to temporarily lose interest on destroying the world. Her evil heart is now warm and somewhat content. Seeing the children alive and well again makes Her-Dark Majesty very happy. However, Evelyn considers this a small triumph upon seeing her precious children being reincarnated. She wants to keep them safe from her dark army. Thus, Evelyn pulls back her army from near the regions and homes of her precious children to prevent them from becoming casualties of her on-going war.

The presence of the children is a blessing to the gods and to humanity. Wherever they are, peace and prosperity flourished. For a country to enjoy even a small measure of peace, the children of Avalon must thrive and free. The greater the numbers of the children, the more prosper a nation. However, the children will not tolerate oppressive rule or society. Thus, they will migrate to a country with openness and free.

PANDEMIC

"I have to stop the world," said GOD, "so that you can make time for yourself. Stop going to the church; stop going to the temple; and stop attending any large gatherings. I want you to focus on yourself and meditate. There are many of you now in the world, and not enough are seeking spirituality. However, you are lacking in quality. A quality I look for is your ability to become enlightenment and more. If you insist on going to these gatherings instead, I will not stop the harmful diseases from infecting you nor will I stop the disturbed people from attacking you. Heed my warning and do consider."

THE END

ABOUT THE AUTHOR

He came to America in 1981. He joined the US-Army in 1992-1996. After the Army, he went on spiritual journey and found spiritual ascension. Then, he moved to Florida in 2008. There, he started writing his first book (THE TREASURES FOR ASCENSION FROM THE GOD OF ALL KNOWING). Thereafter, he published his second book (THE CHILDREN OF AVALON). Up until now, he is the only known ascended being to have written his own books.

Printed in the United States
by Baker & Taylor Publisher Services